To show you care when someone's there, "hello" and "goodbye" are words you can share.

Do you say "hello" when you spill your milk?

Or when you let out a big sneeze?

No! You say "hello" when you meet new people or see friends you already know. Saying "hello" shows that other people are important.

*When someone arrives, you say "hello!"
Then say "goodbye" when it's time to go.*

is "hello" the only way to say hello?

No! There are many ways to welcome someone.

pirates say "ahoy,"

cowboys say "howdy,"

babies smile,

and dogs say rrrufff!

Mostly, though, you say "hi!" or "hello!"

When someone arrives, you say "hello!"
Then say "goodbye" when it's time to go.

Do you **look grumpy** when you say **"hello"**?

Or **sad** so people know you've missed them?

No! Saying "hello" shows you are happy to see someone.

So give your grandma a hug,

shake the mail carrier's hand. And give a friend a big smile!

When someone arrives, you say "hello!"
Then say "goodbye" when it's time to go.

DO you say "goodbye" when someone gives you an ice-cream cone?

No! You say "goodbye" when people are leaving, or when you have to leave.

saying "goodbye" shows you liked being with them and are sad to see them go.

*When someone arrives, you say "hello!"
Then say "goodbye" when it's time to go.*

is "goodbye" the only way to say goodbye?

No! You can also say "cheerio," "ta ta," and "toodle-oo."

Mostly, though, you say "goodbye" or "bye." You can also wave or give someone you love a goodbye hug.

*Ta ta! Bye bye! Farewell! Cheerio!
All of these words say it's time to go!*

Saying "goodbye" can sometimes be sad. But you can remember the good time that you had with the person who is leaving. And think of the fun you will have being together again!

If you become sad when you say "goodbye," just remember the next "hello" or "hi"!